Notting Hill

RICHARD CURTIS

Level 3

Retold by Andy Hopkins

Series Editors: Andy Hopkins and Jocelyn Potter

Pearson Education Limited
Edinburgh Gate, Harlow,
Essex CM20 2JE, England
and Associated Companies throughout the world.

ISBN: 978-1-4058-8199-9

Script version first published by Hodder and Stoughton 1999
New edition first published by Penguin Books 2005
This edition first published by Pearson Education 2008

15

Typeset by Graphicraft Ltd, Hong Kong
Set in 11/14pt Bembo
Printed in China
SWTC/15

Published by Pearson Education Ltd

Every effort has been made to trace the copyright holders and we apologise in advance for any unintentional omissions. We would be pleased to insert the appropriate acknowledgement in any subsequent edition of this publication.

Contents

Introduction

'I live in Notting Hill. You live in Beverly Hills. Everyone in the world knows who you are. My mother doesn't always remember my name.'

'OK. Fine. I understand.' There seemed nothing more to say. But Anna tried one last time. 'It's not real, you know. . . being famous. I'm also just a girl. Standing in front of a boy. Asking him to love her.'

Anna Scott is an American film star. Anna is rich and beautiful and famous all over the world. Everyone wants to know her. The international press reports everything she does.

William Thacker's life is very different. He owns a small travel bookshop in Notting Hill in London. His business is not very successful. He has some very good friends and a very bad lodger, Spike. Spike is untidy and forgetful. He borrows William's clothes and doesn't remember to give him important messages. And he cannot keep a secret.

One day Anna walks into William's bookshop. Both Anna and William are looking for someone special. Will they find love together? Or are the differences in their lives too great? And what part will Spike play in their story?

The film *Notting Hill* was written by Richard Curtis. Curtis studied at Oxford University, then began writing for television shows like *Mr Bean*. His first film success was *Four Weddings and a Funeral* in 1994 and he has written other successful films like *Bean* (1997), *Bridget Jones' Diary* (2001) and *Love Actually* (2003).

Notting Hill was filmed in 1999. It stars Hugh Grant as William, Julia Roberts as Anna and Rhys Ifans as Spike.

Chapter 1 Just Another Wednesday Morning?

It was a fine spring morning. William Thacker was looking out of his window, thinking about life.

'Notting Hill – not a bad place to be,' he thought. On weekdays, there was the market, selling fruit and vegetables from all over the world. At the weekend, even more people crowded into Portobello Road and the streets around it to buy expensive old furniture, paintings and cheap clothes. Then there were the unusual shops, the cafés and restaurants. The streets were always busy, always full of people. But best of all, this was the place where most of his friends now lived.

Notting Hill was like a small village in the middle of a big city. And in this London village, William Thacker had his home. His wife lived in another part of town. Well, she *was* his wife until two years earlier. Then she left him for a man who looked like Harrison Ford. So in the house with the blue front door, William, twenty-eight years old and single, now lived a strange half-life with his Welsh lodger, Spike.

'Hey, can you help me with an important decision?' Spike walked into the room. He was a tall, thin, pale man with dirty yellow hair and untidy clothes. 'I'm going out with the great Janine tonight and I want to wear the right T-shirt.'

'What have you got?' asked William, trying to show interest.

Spike pulled on a T-shirt. On the front, an alien was swimming in a sea of blood above the words *I Love Blood*.

'Well, there's this one?'

'Hmmm . . . I'm not sure it's romantic enough,' William said thoughtfully.

'Yes . . . maybe you're right.' Spike ran up the stairs, still talking. 'I know you'll like this one.'

He came back wearing a second T-shirt. *Take Me!* read the words on the front, in big, black letters.

'Well,' said William slowly, 'will she think you're looking for true love? I'm not sure that she will.'

'Oh, I don't want her to get the wrong idea! OK, just one more.'

He came down in the last T-shirt. Below little red hearts, it read: *You're the most beautiful woman in the world.*

William showed his surprise. 'Yes,' he said. 'That's perfect. Well done!'

'Thanks. Great. I'm feeling lucky!' Spike smiled.

He turned and walked proudly upstairs. On the back of the T-shirt, William could now read: *Let's go to bed.*

'Oh, Spike . . .' he sighed to himself.

It was just another Wednesday, another working day. William walked through the market and opened the door to his shop, The Travel Book Company. It was a small shop that sold . . . well, travel books. But he never seemed to sell many. Inside, there were a few small rooms full of shelves, and every shelf was heavy with books – expensive books, cheap books, large hardbacks and small paperbacks.

William greeted Martin, his assistant. A small man with a beard and a nervous smile, Martin always tried to see the best in life. He liked to please people, but was not very good at selling. In fact, people often thought he was a little strange.

William started looking at some papers on his desk.

'Great. Last week we made nothing! In fact, we lost £347 on those guidebooks to Turkey . . .'

'Oh dear. Never mind. Shall I go and get us some coffee? Make you feel better?' Martin asked, smiling.

As he left for the café, a woman came into the shop. William looked up at her, looked down, thought for a minute, then looked up again. She was a beautiful young woman with long, black hair, dressed simply in a black jacket and trousers. He was sure he knew her. Was it possible? Could it really be her? Yes, it was Anna Scott, the biggest film star in the world! To William – to most men – she was the most beautiful woman on Earth.

He tried to stay calm. 'Can I help you?'

She looked at him through her dark glasses. 'No, thanks. I'll just look around.'

His eyes followed her as she went over to a shelf. She picked out a large, expensive guidebook full of colour photographs.

'That book's really not good . . . er . . . if you're thinking of buying it,' he said, a little nervously.

'Really?'

'Yes, but this one is . . . very good,' he said, picking up one of the smaller books from his desk. 'I think the writer really has been to Turkey.'

'Thanks. I'll think about it,' she smiled.

Suddenly, William noticed something on the small screen on his desk.

'Just a minute, please,' he said. He walked to the back of the shop towards a customer who was hiding between two lines of shelves.

'Er . . . excuse me, sir,' he said to the man.

'Yes?'

'Bad news.'

'What?'

'We've got a camera in this part of the shop.'

'So?'

'So I saw you put that book down your trousers,' William told him.

'What book?'

'The one down your trousers.'

'I haven't got a book down my trousers,' replied the man.

'OK. Listen. We seem to disagree about this. I'll call the police and they can take a look. If I'm wrong, I'm really sorry,' William said patiently.

'Right. Er . . . And if I do have a book down my trousers?' the man asked.

'Well . . . this is what I suggest. I'll go back to my desk. You take the *Cadogan Guide to Bali* from your trousers and put it back on the shelf. Or buy it.'

William walked back to his desk. On the screen, he watched as the book came out of the man's trousers. Then it was back on the shelf. The thief started walking slowly towards the door.

William turned back to Anna. 'Sorry about that.'

She smiled. 'No, that's fine. I was thinking of stealing one too, but now I've changed my mind.' She looked at the copies of the cheaper guidebook on his desk. 'Signed by the writer?'

'Yes,' William said. 'We couldn't stop him. If you can find an unsigned copy, you can probably sell it for a lot of money.'

The thief stopped next to Anna, looking at her with interest.

'Can you sign this for me?' he asked, pulling a dirty piece of paper from his coat.

Anna sighed. 'What's your name?' she asked.

'Rufus.'

She wrote on the piece of paper and gave it back to him. He tried to read her handwriting.

'What does it say?' he asked.

She pointed. 'Well, that's my name. And there it says: *Dear Rufus – I hope the police catch you next time.*'

'Nice,' he smiled. 'Would you like my phone number?'

'I don't think so,' she replied. As the man left the shop, she turned to William. 'I think I'll try this one.' She gave him the large, expensive book and the money for it.

'Oh, right. Maybe it isn't as bad as I thought,' William said. 'Probably quite good. And I'll give you this one free.' He dropped the cheaper guidebook into the same bag. 'Very useful for lighting fires or for making paper hats . . .'

A sudden warm smile lit up her face. She looked carefully at this amusing young man with blue eyes and thick brown hair.

'Thanks,' she said, and left.

Chapter 2 First Kiss – Last Kiss?

William felt empty. 'That's it, then. She's gone. And I'll probably never see her again,' he thought to himself.

'Here's your coffee,' Martin said brightly, as he came back into the shop.

'Thanks. You won't believe who was in here a minute ago.'

'Who? Somebody famous?' Martin asked, excited.

But William suddenly changed his mind. 'Oh . . . er . . . no . . . nobody.'

'Perhaps one day a famous person *will* come in!' said Martin, his eyes shining. 'I saw one of the Beatles once . . . Ringo Starr. Well, I think it was Ringo Starr. I'm not really sure . . . he was quite far away. He had long hair and a beard.'

'Hmmm . . . so you think you saw Ringo, but perhaps you didn't?'

'Er . . . yes, that's right.'

'Maybe it was just a man with long hair and a beard?'

'Yes, maybe.'

'Not a very good story, then, is it?' suggested William. He shook his head and finished his coffee. 'Right . . . another one?'

'Yes. No, let's go crazy! I'll have an orange juice.'

Five minutes later, William left the café and hurried back to the bookshop with the orange juice. But as he turned the corner, he walked straight into a woman. The orange juice ran down her shirt.

'I'm so sorry . . .' He looked up at the woman's face. For the second time that day, it was Anna Scott! 'Oh . . . really, I'm sorry. Here . . .'

'What are you doing?' Anna shouted angrily, as William tried to clean her shirt with a paper towel.

William jumped back. 'Nothing, nothing. Listen, I live across the street. You can wash at my house.'

'No, thank you. I just need to call my driver.' She turned away.

'I also have a phone. In five minutes you can be clean and back on the street again . . .'

She turned and looked at him. 'OK. What does *across the street* mean? How far is your house exactly?'

William pointed. 'It's just there. That's my house. The one with the blue door.'

She looked down at her shirt. Then she looked back up at him. 'Well, OK.'

They walked towards William's house. He opened the door.

'Come in. I'll just . . .'

The house was in a terrible mess. William ran inside in front of her and kicked some shoes under the stairs. He threw away an old pizza and tried to hide some dirty plates.

'I'm afraid it's a bit untidy.'

Anna looked around. Her face showed nothing. Taking the bag of books from her, William pointed towards the stairs.

'The bathroom's up there and there's a phone on the desk in the room next to it.'

She took her other bags and walked upstairs. William ran around the ground floor, clearing the mess.

'Anna Scott is in my house! She's in my bathroom! And look at this place! I'll kill Spike,' he thought.

He heard Anna's feet on the stairs and looked up. She was wearing different clothes now – a black top and skirt. Without the dark glasses, her deep brown eyes shone. She looked wonderful. William stopped and stared. He tried to think of something to say.

'Tea . . . Would you like a cup of tea before you go?'

'No, thanks.'

'Coffee?'

'No.'

'Something cold? Orange juice? No, probably not. Water?'

'Really, no.'

'Something to eat . . . some fruit?'

'No.'

'Do you always say no to everything?'

Anna looked amused. 'No. I must go,' she said. 'Thanks for your help.'

'You're welcome.' He wanted to say more, but he couldn't find the words. 'And I'd like to say . . .' he continued, finally, 'you're wonderful. It's my one chance to say it. When you've read that terrible book, you'll never visit my shop again.'

She looked pleased. 'Thank you.'

William walked her to the front door. 'Nice to meet you. Strange, but nice.'

Anna left, and he closed the door behind her.

'Oh, no!' he thought. '"Strange, but nice"! What was I thinking?'

There was a knock on the door. It was Anna again.

'Oh, hi. Did you forget something?'

'I forgot my books,' said Anna, stepping quickly inside the house.

'Oh, right.'

William ran into the kitchen to get the bag. 'Here they are.'

'Thanks. Well . . .'

They stood near the door again. This time, William felt more comfortable. Then Anna moved forward and kissed him. He could smell her hair; he could feel the smoothness of her skin against his. He couldn't believe it. Anna Scott, the woman of his dreams, was here, in his house, kissing him, William Thacker.

At the worst possible time, a key turned in the lock.

'Oh, no. It's my lodger, Spike! I'm sorry. There's no excuse for him.'

Spike walked in and straight past them towards the kitchen. 'I'm going to get some food,' he called over his shoulder. 'Then I'm going to tell you a story that you won't believe . . .'

Anna looked at William. 'You won't tell anyone about this, will you?'

'Right. No one. I mean, I'll tell myself sometimes. But don't worry . . . I won't believe it.'

He opened the door for her a second time.

'Bye.' She touched his hand lightly. And then she was gone.

William walked slowly back into the kitchen.

'Shall we watch videos tonight? I've got some really great films,' Spike said, between mouthfuls of food.

'Yes,' thought William sadly. 'I've got nothing better to do with my life.'

One of Spike's videos was a film starring Anna Scott. Later that evening, as the two men sat in front of the TV, William remembered the touch of her hand, the smell of her hair.

Spike shook his head at the screen. 'It's hard to believe. Somewhere there's a man who can kiss Anna Scott – any time, anywhere.'

'Yes, she's quite wonderful.'

Chapter 3 Call Me!

A customer came into the bookshop the next morning. William knew Mr Smith well.

'Have you got any books by Dickens?' Mr Smith asked.

William sighed. Not again. 'No,' he said slowly and patiently, 'this is a *travel* bookshop. We only sell *travel* books.'

'Oh. And that new John Grisham book?'

'No, John Grisham doesn't write travel books either.'

'Oh, right. Have you got a copy of *Romeo and Juliet*?'

William looked at Mr Smith, then shouted, 'Martin, your customer!'

Martin came out from behind some shelves with a warm smile on his face. 'Can I help you?' he asked Mr Smith.

As William stared sadly out of the window, a bus went past the shop. On the side was a large picture of Anna in her new film, *Helix*. He couldn't stop thinking about her.

♦

A few days later, William walked into his kitchen.

'Hi, Spike.'

'Hi.'

Spike was never Britain's best-dressed man, but today his clothes were even stranger than usual. He was wearing William's scuba diving suit, with a pair of goggles on his head.

'Er . . . Spike? Why are you wearing my scuba diving suit?'

'No clean clothes.'

'There never will be if you don't wash them sometimes,' William suggested.

'And I was looking around your room and I found this. Great, isn't it? I think I look good in it, eh?'

It was a lovely day and they went outside into the sunshine. Spike, still in the scuba diving suit, tried unsuccessfully to read his newspaper through the goggles.

'There's something wrong with these, William,' he said, pointing to the goggles.

'That's because they were made specially for my eyes. So I can see the fish.'

'Oh, right.'

'So . . . any messages for me?' William asked.

'Yes, I wrote down two.'

'Two. Were there only two messages?'

'You want me to write down all of them?'

William closed his eyes and sighed. 'The ones you didn't write down . . . Who were they from?'

'Mmmm . . . Was there one . . . ? No, it's gone. I just can't remember anything about them. Oh no, wait! Your mother's leg is hurting her again. And don't forget lunch on Saturday.'

'Any others?' asked William hopefully.

'No, that's it. No others.' Spike sat back in his chair and closed his eyes. Then he seemed to remember something. 'Ah . . . but if you want *all* your messages, there was one from an American girl a few days ago. Anna, I think she said.'

William's heart stopped. 'What did she say?'

'Well, it was a bit strange. She said, "Hi, it's Anna." And then she said, "Call me at the Ritz." And then she gave a different name.'

'What was the name?'

'No idea. One name's difficult enough to remember, but two . . .'

William ran inside.

'Hello, is that the Ritz Hotel?' he said, when a man answered the phone.

'Can I help you, sir?'

'Er . . . I hope you can. I'm a friend of Anna Scott. She left me a message. She's staying with you. She asked me to call her.'

'I'm sorry, sir. We have nobody here of that name.'

'No, that's right . . . I know that. She's using another name. She left a message with my lodger – a bad mistake. Think of the stupidest person you know . . . well, my lodger's even worse. He's so stupid . . .'

'Try "Flintstone".'

William looked up from the phone and turned towards Spike. 'What?'

'Try "Flintstone",' Spike repeated.

William spoke slowly into the phone. 'Is it possible that Flintstone means anything to you?'

'I'll put you through, sir.'

William could hear another phone ringing. He tried to stay calm.

'What shall I say?' he thought to himself. He practised a few words. 'Hi. Hi. Anna. Hi.' And then he heard her voice.

'Hi.'

'Oh . . . hi. It's William Thacker. We . . . er . . . I work in a bookshop. You called me . . .'

'Well, yes. Three days ago.'

'I'm so sorry. You probably think . . . It was a mistake. My stupid lodger, Spike, took the message. And he didn't give it to me until now.'

'Oh, OK,' she said slowly.

'Perhaps I could come to the Ritz for . . . tea, or something?'

'Yes, but I'm a little busy today . . .' She was silent for a minute. 'But let's try. Four o'clock.'

'Right, great.' William put down the phone. 'Wonderful.'

Chapter 4 Tea at the Ritz?

William arrived at the Ritz Hotel carrying some roses for Anna. As he got into the lift, another young man followed him in.

'Which floor?' William asked.

'Three.'

The lift stopped at the third floor and William and the young man got out. They both looked around for the room numbers, then they both turned right. Anna, William knew, was in

Room 38. As he walked, the young man followed closely behind him. William looked over his shoulder questioningly. He slowed down at Room 38 . . . and the other man did, too. William pointed at the number.

'Are you sure you . . . ?'

The man smiled. 'Yes,' he replied.

'Oh, right.'

William knocked. A bright-faced American girl opened the door.

'Hello. I'm Karen. Sorry. Everything's taking longer than we thought. Here's all the information you need.'

She gave each of them a press package with pictures from Anna's new film, *Helix*. William looked at the woman, then at the man behind him. What was happening? Then Karen showed them into a large room. William was surprised to see a number of reporters and photographers, all clearly waiting to talk to Anna.

'What did you think of the film?' Karen asked.

'Wonderful,' the man behind William replied. 'A bit of *Close Encounters* – and a lot of *Jean de Florette*.'

They both turned to William for his opinion.

'I agree,' he said quickly.

'I'm sorry . . . Which magazines are you from?' Karen asked.

'I'm Tarquin from *Time Out*.'

'Great. And you?' she asked, looking towards William.

William didn't know what to say. He looked around for ideas and, on a small table, saw a copy of *Horse and Hound* magazine.

'*Horse and Hound*. The name's William Thacker. Miss Scott knows I'm coming.'

'OK. Take a seat. I'll check.'

The two men sat down as Karen went into the next room.

'You've brought her flowers?' said Tarquin with interest.

William thought quickly. 'No . . . No, they're . . . for my

grandmother. She's in a hospital near here. I'm going to see her after this.'

'Oh, I'm sorry. Which hospital?'

William didn't know any of the hospitals in the area. 'Er . . . I don't like to talk about it. I hope you don't mind.'

'Oh, sure. Of course.'

Just then, Karen came back into the room and called his name. 'Mr Thacker? Anna will see you now. You've got five minutes.'

It was a large sitting room filled with flowers. Anna was standing with her back to a window, wearing an expensive suit. Her hair was tied back. William thought again how beautiful she looked.

'Hi.'

'Hello.'

'I brought you these,' he said, holding out the flowers. 'But . . . clearly . . . you've already got some.'

'Oh, no. These are great,' said Anna, taking them.

There was a long silence. William tried to think of something to say.

'Sorry about not ringing back. The two-names idea was difficult for my stupid lodger to understand.'

'No, *I'm* sorry. I try to stay private, so I always choose a name from a children's film. Last time I came to England, I was Mrs Bambi.'

Karen's boss came into the room.

'Everything OK?' he asked Anna.

'Yes thanks, Jeremy.'

'And you're from *Horse and Hound* magazine?' he asked William.

Anna looked at William. 'Really? *Horse and Hound*?' She smiled.

She sat down. The room fell silent. She and Jeremy were looking towards William, waiting.

'Right,' he said, taking a seat. 'I'll just start, then?' He tried to imagine being a reporter for *Horse and Hound* magazine. What did his readers want to know? 'Right. Er . . . the film's excellent. But . . . did you ever think of having more horses in it?' he asked hesitantly.

Jeremy looked at William and sighed.

'Well,' started Anna, trying to be serious, 'we wanted more horses . . . but it was difficult. I mean, there aren't many horses on Mars.'

'Yes, Mars. Of course . . . very difficult.'

Jeremy stared at William. Then he looked at Anna, but she seemed happy. He left the room.

William put his head in his hands. 'I'm sorry. I arrived outside and they gave me this press package. I didn't know what to do.'

'No, *I'm* sorry. They gave me a timetable for this and it ended at four. Listen, I just want to say that I'm sorry for the other day . . . the kissing thing. I don't know why I did it. I wanted to make sure you were OK about it.'

'Is that all she wants to say?' William thought. He felt hurt, but tried to hide it. 'Yes,' he said. 'No problem. Of course, that's fine.'

Jeremy came back into the room and the two fell silent.

'Don't forget to ask Miss Scott about her next film,' Jeremy said helpfully.

'Oh, yes. Excellent. Er . . . Any horses in that one? Or hounds?'

Anna looked at him, amused. 'It takes place under water.'

'Right.'

Jeremy left the room again.

William watched him go, then turned back to Anna. 'I'm sorry. Things like this only happen in dreams, not in real life. Good dreams, of course . . . It's a dream to see you.'

'And what happens next in the dream?' Anna asked.

'Well . . .' William started, 'in the dream, I just become a different person, a better person, because you can do that in dreams. Then I walk across the room and kiss the girl. But in real life you know it'll never happen.'

The door opened again.

'That's it,' Jeremy said. 'No more time, I'm afraid. Did you get what you wanted?'

'Nearly,' William replied, looking at Anna.

'OK . . . maybe one more question.'

He left the room.

'Are you busy tonight?' William asked Anna.

'Yes.'

Jeremy came back in. William and Anna stood and shook hands.

'It was nice to meet you, Mr Thacker.' She smiled. 'Strange, but nice.'

'Thank you. You are *Horse and Hound*'s favourite actress. You and Black Beauty*.'

Tarquin was waiting outside. 'How was she?' he asked.

'Wonderful.'

'Wait a minute!' Tarquin said in surprise. 'She took your grandmother's flowers?'

William thought quickly. 'Yes, that's right. What a pig!'

He turned towards the lift, but Karen called out to him.

'This way, Mr Thacker. You can talk to the others now.'

'The others?' thought William.

He found himself in another room with the male star of *Helix*.

'Pleased to meet you. Did you enjoy the film?' the star asked.

'Oh yes . . . very much. Er . . . did you enjoy making the film?'

'I did.'

'Which bits did you most enjoy making?'

'Well, you tell me which bits you liked. Then I'll tell you if I liked making them.'

* Black Beauty: a horse in a famous children's book, and in television programmes and films of the story

'Hmmm,' said William thoughtfully. 'I liked the bit on Mars very much. Did you enjoy that bit?'

The male star stared at William. He ended the discussion as quickly as he could.

Five minutes later, William found himself with an actor who spoke no English. Luckily, next to him was a woman who did.

William felt more comfortable with his questions now. 'Did you have a deep understanding of the person you were playing?'

The woman asked the question in Spanish and waited for the actor's answer.

'No.'

'No,' she said to William.

'And why not?' asked William.

The woman put the question in Spanish and waited for the answer. It was quite long.

'Because he played a crazy man-eating alien.'

Another room. A child actress this time. She was eleven years old.

'Is this your first film?'

'No. It's my twenty-second.'

'Of course it is,' William said in surprise. 'Er . . . any favourites out of the twenty-two?'

'Working with Leonardo.'

'Da Vinci?'

She looked at him strangely. 'DiCaprio.'

Finally, the bad dream seemed to be ending. William walked towards the lift again, pushing past the cameramen.

'Mr Thacker!' It was Karen. William sighed deeply. 'Have you got a minute?'

And then he was back in the room with Anna.

'That thing I was doing tonight . . . I've changed my plans. I have to spend the evening with *Horse and Hound*'s star reporter.' Anna smiled.

William's heart jumped. 'Oh well, great. Excellent.' Then he had a sudden thought. 'Oh, no! It's my sister's birthday... we're having dinner!'

'OK. Fine.'

'But no, I won't go.'

'No, I mean, if it's fine with you, I'll come too,' she said.

'You'll come with me to my sister's birthday party?'

'If that's all right?'

'Of course it's all right. My friend Max is cooking and he's the worst cook in the world. But you can hide the food in your bag . . .'

'OK.'

'OK.'

Chapter 5 The Birthday Party

Max was busy preparing the meal. 'He's bringing a girl?' he asked his wife, Bella. 'Are you serious?'

'Yes. Quite a surprise, isn't it?'

'Does the girl have a name?'

'He didn't say.'

Black smoke was pouring from the oven. 'Oh no! What's happening here?' said Max, running towards it. Then the doorbell rang and he ran to the door. He threw it open. 'Come in, come in! Food problems!' And he ran back to the oven.

William and Anna walked into the large kitchen.

'Hi! Sorry – he's finding the meat a bit difficult,' said Bella, welcoming her guests from her wheelchair.

'Hi,' said Anna.

Bella looked at her carefully. 'Hey! You look like . . .'

'Bella, this is Anna,' William said quickly.

'Right,' she replied, looking carefully at Anna's face.

'OK, I've solved the problem,' said Max, turning back from the oven. 'Hello, Anna!' He stopped in surprise as he saw her face. 'Er . . . Have some wine.'

'Thank you.'

The doorbell rang again and Max went to the front door.

'Happy Birthday! You look wonderful,' he said, as Honey hurried in.

Honey, a small young woman with a big smile and large eyes, danced around happily, showing her new dress. Max followed her to the kitchen.

'Listen,' he whispered. 'Your brother has brought this girl and . . . er . . .'

They reached the kitchen.

'Hi, everyone!' Honey smiled to the others. Then she suddenly saw Anna. 'Oh, wow!'

William spoke quickly. 'Honey, this is Anna. Anna, this is Honey. She's my baby sister.'

'Hi,' said Anna with a smile.

'Oh, wow! This is one of those really important times in a person's life. I know I should be calm about it. But Anna, I love you! I think you're the most beautiful woman on Earth. And I have honestly believed for some time that we could be best friends. What do you think?' Anna looked surprised and amused, but pleased. 'Marry Will!' Honey continued. 'He's really nice, and then we can be sisters.'

'I'll think about it,' Anna laughed.

The doorbell rang again.

'That'll be Bernie,' said Max, going to the door.

A large man with a round, pleasant face walked in.

'Sorry I'm late, Max. I made a mess at work again, I'm afraid. Lost millions.'

'Bernie! Come in. This is Anna.'

'Hello, Anna. Glad to meet you.' He shook her hand, then

turned to Honey. 'Happy Birthday, Honey Bunny! Here you are.' He gave her his present. 'It's a hat. You don't have to wear it.'

Max poured Bernie a drink. Then he and William went to prepare the table. Max took his drink and joined Anna.

'So tell me, Anna, what do you do?'

'I'm an actress.'

'Great. I'm a stockbroker. But I've done a little bit of theatre in my time. Not as a job, of course. I always thought it was a difficult life, acting. I mean, the money's terrible, isn't it?'

Anna agreed. 'It can be.'

Bernie continued. 'I know friends from university – clever people – and they earn very little. Seven, eight thousand pounds a year. What sort of acting do you do?'

'Films, mainly.'

'Oh, excellent. Well done.' Bernie seemed more interested. 'How's the pay in films? The last film you made . . . What were you paid?'

'Fifteen million dollars.'

Bernie's face went bright red. 'Right. Right. So that's . . . quite good. Very good, really. Er . . . can I get you another drink?'

'I think we're ready,' called Max, walking towards the table.

Anna looked around, then asked Bella, 'Could you tell me where the . . .'

'It's just down there, on the right,' she said, pointing.

'I'll show you,' offered Honey.

'Quickly, quickly – talk very quickly. What are you doing here with Anna Scott?' Bella said to William after Anna and Honey left the room. The others crowded around them.

'Anna Scott?' said Bernie, turning pale. 'The film star?'

'Yes.'

'Oh, no . . .'

Honey returned to the kitchen, and said in a whisper, 'I don't believe it! I walked into the toilet with her. I was still talking when she started taking off her jeans. She had to ask me to leave.'

The meal was very enjoyable. The old friends laughed and joked together, and Anna soon felt part of the group.

'What do you think of the meat, Anna?' asked Bella.

Anna answered in a whisper, so Max couldn't hear. 'I don't usually eat meat . . .' She smiled.

Bella put her hand to her mouth. 'Oh, no!' she laughed.

They moved into the sitting room for coffee.

'Anna, you have done so much and we have clearly failed in life,' Max said. 'That's not a bad thing. In fact, we should be proud of it. I'm going to give the last piece of cake to the person who has the saddest life.' Max looked around.

There was a short silence. Then William looked at Bernie.

Bernie went first. 'Well, it's me, isn't it? I do a job that I don't understand. I haven't had a girlfriend since I was twelve. And if I get any fatter, I probably never will.'

'*I* like you,' Honey told him. 'Well, I did, before you got so fat.'

Max turned to Bernie. 'You see. And you also earn a lot of money. Honey here earns almost nothing for working long hours in London's worst record shop.'

'That's true. And I've got strange hair and funny, goggly eyes. I only seem to go out with men who are unkind. And no one will ever marry me . . .'

'You see, Honey is terribly sad,' said Max.

'But her best friend is Anna Scott,' Bella added.

'That's true,' Honey agreed. 'She needs me. What can I say?'

'And her legs work,' continued Bella, 'while I'm in this wheelchair, day and night. And even worse, I've given up smoking, my favourite thing. And the fact is,' she said hesitantly, 'we can't have a baby.'

The room was completely silent now.

'Bella!' said William.

'No! It's not true!' Bernie said sadly.

‘That’s life. We’re lucky in lots of ways, but surely I get the cake?’ Bella asked.

Max lightened the conversation. ‘Well, I don’t know. Look at William. Very unsuccessful at work. A failed marriage. He *was* handsome, but is now losing his good looks. And it’s clear that he’ll never hear from Anna again. Not when she knows that he was called Floppy at school.’

They all laughed loudly.

‘Ah, so I get the cake?’ suggested William.

Max answered. ‘I think you do, yes.’

William reached for the cake.

‘Wait a minute. What about me?’ It was Anna.

‘You?’ asked Max.

The others stared at her.

‘Well, I’d like to try for the cake.’

‘You’ll have to prove it,’ William smiled. ‘It’s a lovely cake and I’m going to fight you for it.’

‘Well . . . I’ve worried about my weight since I was nineteen. So I’ve been hungry for ten years. I’ve had a lot of not nice boyfriends, and one of them hit me. And every time my heart’s broken, the press write about it. Oh, and it costs me millions to look like this.’

‘Really,’ said Honey, looking closely at her face.

‘Really. And one day, not long from now . . .’ The table was silent again. It was clear that Anna was speaking from the heart. ‘ . . . my looks will go. They’ll realize I can’t act. And I’ll become a sad middle-aged woman who was famous for a few years,’ she continued sadly.

They all looked at Anna in silence. Then Max broke the silence with a shout.

‘No – nice try, beautiful, but you must think we’re stupid!’

They all laughed.

‘Useless!’ said William to Anna. ‘You’re not getting the cake!’

When it was time to leave, William and Anna stood up.

'That was a great evening,' Anna said to Max.

'Thank you so much for coming,' he replied warmly.

'And I have to say that I love your tie, Max.' It was blue with red telephone boxes on it.

'Now I know you're lying.'

Anna turned to Bella. 'Lovely to meet you.'

'And you. It's a pity you don't eat meat. But don't worry – I won't tell Max.' Bella looked at her husband with a smile.

'What? Oh, no!'

'Goodnight, Honey,' said Anna.

'I'm so sorry about the toilet thing. I meant to leave but I just . . . Listen, ring me if you need to go shopping with someone. I know lots of nice, cheap places. Of course, money isn't really . . . Nice to meet you.' Honey gave her a kiss.

'You too. I'll come to you for help with all my clothes!'

'Love your work,' said Bernie, smiling nervously.

As the front door closed behind them, William and Anna heard the others scream with excitement.

'Sorry,' William said. 'They always do that when I leave the house . . .'

'Floppy?' she laughed.

He looked at her. 'It's my hair! It was always falling across my face.'

'Why is Bella in a wheelchair?'

'It was an accident – about eighteen months ago.' There was pain in William's eyes at the memory.

'And the baby thing – is that a result of the accident?'

'I'm not sure. I don't think they've tried for children before.'

They walked in silence, a comfortable silence. It was a lovely night.

'Would you like to come . . . ? My house is just . . . ?' William asked hesitantly.

She smiled and shook her head. 'It's too difficult.'

'OK. That's fine.'

'Are you busy tomorrow?' she asked.

'I thought you were leaving.'

'I was.'

They were walking along a street with trees on one side.

'What's in there?' asked Anna, pointing to the trees.

'A garden. All these squares have gardens in the middle for the people around them. They're like little villages.'

'Let's go in.'

'Ah, no. They're private. They're only for the people who live here.'

'And you always follow the rules?' she asked. She seemed very interested in his answer.

'Me? Er . . . oh no, not me. I do what I want.' In fact, William *was* the kind of person who always followed rules. But he started to climb the locked metal gate. He fell back. 'Oh dear . . .' He tried again, and again he fell. 'It's more difficult than it looks, Anna.'

'Stand back,' Anna replied, starting to climb. She was over the gate in a second. 'Your turn, Floppy!'

At last, with great difficulty, William succeeded in climbing over. He jumped down inside the garden.

'What's in this garden that's so good?'

Then, in the silence of the garden, under the trees, she reached out and kissed him. This time it was a real kiss.

'Nice garden!' he said, in surprise.

As they walked around on the grass, they came to a wooden seat. She read the words on it, '*June loved this garden. Joseph always sat here with her.*' The dates below it read: *June Wetherby 1917–1992*. 'You see, some people do spend all their lives together,' Anna said quietly.

William looked deeply into her eyes. He spoke softly. 'Yes, they do.'

Chapter 6 Room Service

The following evening, William was getting ready to go out. As usual, he was late.

'Spike? Have you seen my glasses?'

'No, I'm afraid not,' Spike answered, his eyes on the TV.

'Oh, no! Where are they? This happens every time I go to the cinema. Usually there are glasses everywhere. But when I really need them, they disappear. It's one of life's little jokes.'

William ran upstairs, then came down again.

'Right, I've got to go,' he called to Spike. 'Thanks very much for your help!'

'You're welcome. Did you find them?'

'No.'

As the door closed behind William, Spike moved on the sofa. Was he sitting on something? He reached down and pulled out William's glasses.

At the cinema, William looked a little strange as he sat next to Anna – beautiful Anna! – in his scuba diving goggles.

After the film, they decided to go for a meal in a Japanese restaurant.

'So who left who?' Anna asked.

'*She* left *me*,' replied William.

'Why?'

'She finally saw what I was really like.'

'Oh. That's not good.'

They could hear loud conversation from a table just around the corner from theirs.

'No, no, no. I'll take Anna Scott,' said a man's voice.

William and Anna listened carefully.

A second man disagreed. 'I didn't like her last film. I fell asleep ten minutes after it started.'

The first man spoke again. 'I don't really mind what the films are like. I just like watching her.'

'No, she's not my type. I prefer the other one. The one who gets excited every time you take her out for a cup of coffee.'

Anna looked at William. 'Meg Ryan,' she mouthed silently.

'You know,' said the first voice again, 'some girls don't let you near them. But Anna isn't like that. You know she wants it. She's the same as all actresses. Someone you can just . . .'

Anna's smile disappeared.

'Right, that's enough,' William said, standing up. He walked over to the men's table. There were four of them.

'I'm sorry, but . . .'

'Can I help you?' one of the men said politely.

'Well, I was listening to your conversation – I couldn't help it. But you know, you're talking about a real person. And you shouldn't talk about her like that . . .'

'Oh, go away. Who are you – her father?' The men laughed loudly.

Anna came up behind William and pulled him away. The men at the table didn't see her face and continued laughing.

'I'm sorry,' William said to her.

'It's OK. I love the fact you tried.' They started walking towards the door of the restaurant. Then Anna stopped. 'No, give me a minute.' And she walked back to the men's table.

'Hi!' She smiled sweetly. 'I'm sorry about my friend.'

'Oh . . .' said the man who was doing most of the talking. He knew her face immediately. 'Listen, I'm sorry.'

'Please, please,' she said. 'Stop there. I'm sure it was all just friendly talk. It didn't mean anything. And I'm sure you can't help being stupid. Enjoy your meal. The fish is really good.'

She walked back to William, still smiling. The men sat in silence, their mouths hanging open.

Outside the restaurant Anna said, 'Why did I do that?'

'It was wonderful.'

'No, I'm stupid and . . . What am I doing with you?'

'I don't know, I'm afraid,' he replied, smiling.

'I don't know, either,' she said softly.

They arrived at the front door of the Ritz.

'Do you want to come up?' she asked quietly.

'There seem to be lots of reasons why I shouldn't.'

'There *are* lots of reasons. But do you want to come up?'

His look said yes.

'Give me five minutes,' she smiled, and walked towards the lift.

For William, time seemed to pass very slowly. The hands on his watch refused to move.

Exactly five minutes later, he knocked at the door of her room. She opened it. 'Hi.' Something seemed to be wrong.

'Hi,' said William, kissing her. 'It's wonderful to be able to do that.'

Anna's eyes were wide and there was a very serious look on her face. 'You have to go,' she whispered.

'Why?'

'My boyfriend. I thought he was in America. But in fact, he's in the next room.'

'Your boyfriend?' William couldn't believe it.

'Who is it?' The man was standing in the doorway, behind Anna, now. Jeff was a famous film star. Handsome, too – women all over the world dreamt about him.

William thought quickly. 'Room service.'

'How are you doing? I thought you people always wore suits?' Jeff said in a friendly way.

'Well, yes . . . but I've just changed because I'm going home. This is my last call.'

'Oh, great. Could I have some really cold water up here?'

'I'll see what I can do.'

'And maybe you could clear these dirty plates while you're here?'

William calmly picked up the dirty plates.

'Really, don't do that,' Anna said nervously. 'I'm sure that's not his job,' she told Jeff.

'Is there a problem?' Jeff asked William.

'No, no. It's fine.'

'What's your name?' he asked

'It's . . . er . . . Bernie.'

'Well, thank you, Bernie,' he said, pushing five pounds into William's hand. Jeff turned to Anna. 'Hey! Good surprise or bad surprise?'

Anna looked uncomfortable. 'Nice surprise.'

Jeff kissed her.

'She's lying,' he said to William. 'She hates surprises.' He turned to Anna. 'So what food are you ordering?'

'I haven't decided.'

'Well, don't order too much. I don't want people saying, "There goes that famous actor with the big, fat girlfriend,"' Jeff laughed, leaving the room.

William looked at Anna. 'I think I should leave. This is all very strange. I didn't realize . . .'

'I'm so sorry. I don't know what to say.'

'I think "goodbye" is probably the right word.'

William walked downstairs and out into the lonely night. His heart ached.

Chapter 7 Alone Again

William looked out of the window of his house, lost in his thoughts.

'Talk to me, William. This is me, Spikey. Tell me what's wrong.'

William never usually spoke about his feelings. But this time he needed to talk to someone – even if it had to be Spike!

'Well, OK. There's a girl . . .' he began hesitantly.

'Aha! A girl. I thought so. Speak, friend.'

'She's someone who . . . can never be mine. I've been close to her, but I can never be as close again. And I really miss her.'

Spike looked thoughtful. 'Yes. That's a problem. I missed a girl at Swansea station once. I got the time wrong. I left five minutes before the train arrived!' He laughed.

'Thanks,' William sighed. 'Very helpful.'

That night, William ate with his friends at Tony's restaurant. They were the only people there, as usual. They often ate there, because Tony was an old friend. This was his first restaurant. He was trying hard to make it a success.

On the front page of Bernie's newspaper was a picture of Anna and Jeff at Heathrow Airport.

'You didn't know she had a boyfriend?' Max found this hard to believe.

'No. Did you?' William asked, surprised. The looks on their faces showed that everyone knew. 'You all knew? My life is destroyed because I don't read *Hello* magazine?'

'Anna's a big star. She's world-famous, and you're just an ordinary person. It's unimaginable. But don't worry! I have the answer to your problems . . .' Everyone looked at Max with interest. 'Her name is Tessa and she works in our office. She's a bit strange, but she's very clever and her kisses are unbelievable.' Bella put her head on one side and looked at him. 'Well, that's what people tell me,' he finished quickly.

◆

So a few days later, the friends sat together again at the dinner table in Max and Bella's kitchen. William was worried.

The doorbell rang. As Max answered the door, the others could hear the visitor's loud, excited voice.

'I got lost. I didn't know where I was! Everything around here has the word "Kensington" in it – Kensington Park Road, Kensington Gardens, Kensington Park Gardens . . .'

Max introduced the visitor as they came into the kitchen. 'Tessa, this is Bella, my wife.'

'Oh, you're in a wheelchair,' said Tessa brightly.

'That's right.'

'And this is William,' Max continued.

'Hello, William. Max has told me *everything* about you,' she laughed.

'Has he?' replied William nervously.

'Some wine, Tessa?' Max offered.

'Oh, yes please. Let's get drunk, Willie!'

William looked even more worried.

◆

A few weeks after Tessa's visit, Max and Bella had another dinner party. This time they invited a woman called Keziah to meet William. She was pale and thin, and she sat nervously at the table.

'Meat, Keziah?' Max asked, reaching for her plate.

'No, thank you. I only eat fruit.'

Max and Bella looked at her, and then at William.

'Only fruit?' William asked.

'I believe that fruit and vegetables have feelings. So cooking hurts them. I only eat things that have fallen from the tree. Then they're already dead,' Keziah explained.

'Right. Right. Very interesting. So these potatoes . . .'

' . . . were murdered. Yes.'

'Murdered? Poor potatoes. Terrible,' agreed William. 'Oh, when will this evening end?' he thought to himself.

◆

So Tessa and Keziah came and went. Neither was a success, but Max didn't give up. A month later, Rosie sat at the table with William,

Bella, and Max. Rosie seemed very nice. She was pretty and well-dressed, and there was nothing unusual about her. She seemed intelligent and friendly. To his surprise, William even liked her.

'Great coffee!' she said.

'Thank you. I'm sorry about the meat,' Max said.

'Don't be sorry. I thought it was really... interesting.'

'"Interesting" means terrible,' suggested William.

'Yes, you're right. Really terrible,' she replied.

They all laughed.

'Maybe we'll meet again some time,' she said to William, as she was leaving.

'Yes. That sounds . . . great.'

'Well?' asked Bella, when they were alone.

'She's perfect – perfect,' William replied.

'But . . . ?' Bella looked at him carefully.

William spoke quietly. 'I think you've forgotten. It's difficult to find someone you love. Someone who will also love you. The chances are very small. Look at me. Except for the American, I've only loved two girls in my life. And both times it ended badly.'

'That's not fair,' Max said.

'No, really. One of them left our marriage more quickly than you can say "Indiana Jones". The other,' he said, looking at Bella, 'married my best friend.'

'But she still loves you.' Bella smiled at him.

'Yes, as a sister loves a brother . . .'

'Well, I never wanted you in any other way!' They all laughed. 'I mean, I loved you – you were terribly funny. But when you kissed my ears . . .'

William spoke quickly. 'And thirty years from now, I'm still going to be alone.'

'Do you want to stay the night?' Bella asked.

'Why not? At home there's just a crazy Welshman waiting for me!'

As the evening came to an end, Max carried Bella upstairs to bed. William sat in a chair, eyes wide open, feeling very lonely.

Chapter 8 Behind the Blue Door

The following morning, William walked home. He thought about Max and Bella and how much in love they were. And he thought about his own life. What was he doing? Where was he going?

He arrived home and got ready for work. As he was looking in the mirror, the doorbell rang.

'Who's that at this time of day?' he thought. 'Probably the postman.' He went downstairs to answer it.

He opened the door, and his heart jumped. It wasn't the postman – it was a beautiful woman in dark glasses. Unbelievable.

'Can I come in?' Anna asked.

'Come in.'

Her hair was a mess and she looked tired and unhappy. But to William, she looked wonderful.

He took her into the kitchen and Anna poured out her story.

'The photos were taken years ago,' Anna explained. 'I was poor... It happens a lot. That's not an excuse, I know. But it's worse than that. While one man was taking photos, another man was filming me. I didn't know anything about that. Now it looks like a dirty sex film. And, well, they've sold the pictures and they're everywhere.' Anna looked ready to cry. William shook his head.

'And now I don't know where to go,' Anna continued. 'There are crowds of reporters outside the hotel. I just need to get away from them.'

'This is the place,' William said calmly.

'Thank you,' she said quietly. 'I'm only in London for two

days. But the British press are so . . . It's the worst place to be.' She was very unhappy. 'They're terrible pictures. They make me look like . . .'

'Don't think about it. Now, would you like tea? A bath?'

'Oh yes, a bath.'

Five minutes later, Spike came in through the front door, looking excitedly at the pictures of Anna in his newspaper.

'Wow! Look at that! Wonderful!' he said to himself, as he walked upstairs.

He opened the bathroom door, still reading. He went over to the toilet without taking his eyes off the newspaper.

'Are you Spike?' a voice said from behind him.

Spike looked up, then turned his head slowly. He couldn't believe his eyes. There, in the bath, was Anna Scott! He quickly left the bathroom, calmed himself down, then opened the door again.

Anna saw his face come slowly round the door, his mouth hanging open.

'Hi,' she said, smiling.

'I just wanted to be sure.' Spike backed out and closed the door again. 'Oh thank you, thank you,' he whispered, closing his eyes.

After her bath, Anna looked calmer.

'I'm really sorry about last time,' she said to William in the sitting room. 'Jeff just flew in. I thought we were finished.'

'No, that's fine. I don't often get the chance to clear away the dirty plates of a Hollywood star. I enjoyed it very much. How is he?'

'I don't know. One day, I couldn't remember any of the reasons that I loved him. And how are you – and love?'

'Well, there's a question . . . without an interesting answer.'

'I *have* thought about you,' she said, looking into his eyes.

'Oh no, no . . . no.' William's heart ached. It was too painful. He didn't want her to continue. But she did.

'But there's a problem. When I try to be with someone ordinary, it never works.'

'Of course, I completely understand. Thank you for telling me that.' William felt uncomfortable and changed the subject. 'Is that the film you're doing?' he asked, pointing to some papers in her hand.

'Yes. We start filming in Los Angeles on Tuesday.'

'Would you like me to help you learn your lines?'

'Will you?' She looked pleased. 'It's all talk, talk, talk.'

'What's the story about?'

'I'm a difficult but clever young officer who, in about twenty minutes, will save the world.'

'Well done, you!'

William found the language of the film almost impossible to understand. But he read the other parts for Anna, and she practised her lines. They had great fun. As the day passed, Anna seemed to forget about her problems.

'So what do you think of the film?' she asked, when they stopped.

'Exciting. It's not Jane Austen or Henry James. But it is exciting.'

'You think I should do Henry James?'

'I'm sure you'd be great in Henry James. But . . . I mean . . . this writer's quite good, too.'

'Yes,' she said. 'Nobody in *The Wings of the Dove* says, "Tell the Pentagon we need black star cover!" '

'And I think that's a pity.'

Anna smiled her widest smile. He really was helping.

Later that evening, they sat down to eat.

'I can't believe you have that picture on the wall,' she said, looking at a cheap copy of a Chagall painting.

'You like Chagall?' he asked.

'I do. That's how love should feel. A big, dark blue sky . . .'

'With a fish falling from it.'

'Yes. Happiness isn't happiness without a fish falling from the sky.'

Spike brought pizzas to the table. 'Right. For the Queen of Notting Hill, Carnival Calypso – hot chicken and fruit . . . and a little more chicken.'

'Great,' said Anna, looking at her plate.

'Spike, did I tell you that Anna doesn't eat meat?'

'Ah . . . well, I've got some vegetable soup from last week. If I take off the skin, it'll be perfect.'

After the meal, Spike left to meet his friends in the pub. William and Anna were alone, at last.

'You've got big feet,' Anna said.

'Yes, I've always had them.'

'You know what they say about men with big feet?'

'No, what's that?'

'Big feet . . .' She stopped and looked him in the eye. 'Big shoes!'

They both laughed, comfortably.

A little later, they discussed Anna's film work.

'When I make films,' she told him, 'I don't take my clothes off – well, not all of them. That's the agreement. And they have to discuss it with me if they want to use another person's body in my place.'

'Another person's body? What do you mean?'

'Well, if they want me to show my bottom, I refuse. Another actor has to do it.'

'And do you choose a better bottom than yours?'

'Of course. That's really important.' She laughed.

'What a job!' said William. 'What do those people put on their passports? Profession – Mel Gibson's bottom!'

'Mel uses his own bottom,' Anna said, taking another mouthful of ice-cream. 'It's great.'

'The ice-cream or Mel Gibson's bottom?'

'Both.'

They had a wonderful evening but, of course, it had to end. William walked with Anna up to the bedroom.

'Today has been a good day. Thank you,' said Anna gratefully.

They stopped outside the bedroom door.

'Well . . . thank *you*. Time for bed . . . and the sofa-bed for me.'

'Right.' She kissed him sweetly. Then she went into the bedroom and closed the door. William walked slowly downstairs for a lonely night on the sofa-bed.

He couldn't sleep. He lay there with his eyes wide open. 'Will she come?' He waited and hoped. But nothing happened. Then, suddenly, he heard a sound on the stairs. William waited nervously.

'Hello?' he said into the darkness.

A bearded face looked into the room. 'Hello. Have you got a minute?'

'Spike!'

'Listen. Anna's not with her boyfriend now, is she?' Spike asked.

'No, I don't think so.'

'And she's in your house?'

'Yes.'

'And you like her?'

'Yes.'

'And *she* likes *you*?'

'Yes.'

'Well, isn't this your big chance? You should be up there, with her.' Spike pointed upstairs.

'No, Spike. She's in trouble. This is not the time,' William said angrily.

'All right . . . all right. I understand that.' Spike turned to go. Then he spoke again. 'Do you mind if I try?'

'Spike!'

'No, you're right.'

'I'll talk to you in the morning.' William lay down again.

'OK . . . OK. But maybe it'll be too late then.' Spike went back to bed.

William lay in bed, thinking. A few minutes later, he heard footsteps on the stairs again.

'Oh, go away, will you?' he said angrily.

'OK,' replied Anna quietly.

William jumped up. 'No . . . no. Wait. I thought you were Spike. I'm so happy you're not.'

They stood face to face in the half-light. He kissed her neck softly, then her shoulder. Then he looked at her face. That face. He couldn't believe he was touching Anna Scott.

'Wow!'

'What?' Anna asked.

'Oh, nothing.' And he kissed her deeply.

♦

The next morning, they lay in bed together.

'It's wonderful . . . and strange . . . that I, William Thacker, can look at your naked body.'

'You and every other person in this country,' she replied.

'Oh, yes . . . sorry.'

'Rita Hayworth* always said, "They go to bed with Gilda and they wake up with me." Do you feel that?' she asked.

'Who was Gilda?'

'Her most famous part. Men went to bed with the dream and woke up with the reality. Do you feel that way with me?'

'You're lovelier this morning than you have ever been,' he replied.

* Rita Hayworth: a beautiful Hollywood film star. Her most famous films were made in the 1940s and 1950s.

Anna smiled. 'Oh!' Then she jumped out of bed. 'I'll be back. Don't go away.'

Ten minutes later, Anna returned with breakfast.

'Breakfast in bed.' She smiled warmly. She sat on the bed and asked hesitantly, 'Can I stay a bit longer?'

William looked at her. 'Stay forever,' he said softly.

'Oh, I forgot the sugar.' Just then, the doorbell rang. 'You get the door, I'll get the sugar,' she said, leaving the room.

William sighed. He pulled on his underpants and went downstairs.

'OK, I'm coming,' he shouted. He opened the door and was suddenly caught in the light of lots of cameras. The street was full of reporters, shouting. He quickly shut the door again. 'Jesus Christ!'

'What is it?' Anna called.

'Don't ask,' replied William, his voice shaking.

'William, what is it?' Anna thought he was joking. She went to the door, opened it and looked outside.

'Oh, no . . .' she cried, throwing the door shut. She turned to William. 'And they got a photo of you dressed like that?'

'Undressed like this. Yes.'

Spike walked into the kitchen, naked except for a pair of dirty grey underpants.

'Good morning, my lovely ones,' he greeted them, giving William a big smile.

Anna was on the phone. 'They're outside – hundreds of them. Yes, I know – just get me out of here.'

She put the phone down and walked angrily upstairs.

'Don't go outside, Spike,' said William. 'Really. . . it's not a good idea.'

'Why not?'

'Just don't.' William followed Anna upstairs.

Spike thought for a minute, then he opened the front door.

The air was filled with people shouting, cameras and lights.

'Wow!' thought Spike, standing there in his grey underpants. He liked this! He turned to offer the photographers the best view of his naked body.

When he closed the door, he looked at himself in the mirror. 'Not bad. Not at all bad. Well chosen underpants. Girls love grey.'

William was upstairs, standing in the bedroom doorway.

'How are you doing?' he asked.

'How do you *think* I'm doing?' Anna shouted.

'I don't know what happened.'

'Well, *I* do!' she said, throwing her things into a bag. 'Your stupid friend decided to make some money. So he talked to some reporters!'

'Spike? No, that's not true,' William answered.

'Really? Reporters from every British newspaper are outside your house. They all woke up this morning and thought, "*I* know where that Anna Scott is. She's in the house with the blue front door, in Notting Hill." And then you go out half naked. Unbelievable!'

Spike put his head around the door. 'And *I* went out in *my* underpants, too!'

'Get out, Spike,' William said. 'Listen, Anna, I'm so sorry.'

'I came here to you for protection from these people. And now things are even worse than before! What will everyone think? I mean, I've got a boyfriend . . .' she shouted.

'Have you?' asked William quietly.

'Well, everyone thinks I have. And now there'll be pictures of you in every paper from here to Timbuktu!'

'I know, I know. But . . . just . . . let's stay calm.'

'*You* can stay calm. Everything's fine for you. Everyone will say, "Well done, you. You slept with a film star – we've seen the pictures." '

William looked hurt. 'That is so unfair,' he said seriously.

'You can use it for your business. "Buy a boring book from the man who slept with Anna Scott." '

She pushed past him and out of the room.

'Stop. Please . . . calm down. Have a cup of tea.'

But she refused to listen. 'I don't *want* a stupid cup of tea! I want to go home,' she shouted, running downstairs.

William followed her.

The doorbell rang.

'It's a big car,' Spike called down from the upstairs window. 'It looks like your driver, Anna.'

Anna was a little calmer now, but as cold as ice. 'Tell Spike to buy you an expensive meal – or a holiday,' she said to William. 'I'm sure he has the money now.'

'That's not true. Spike's not like that. And wait a minute . . . this is all crazy. Can't we laugh about it? Terrible things happen in the world . . . Compared to them, this is nothing.'

Spike came downstairs. 'He's going to tell you about people without food in Africa,' he said to Anna.

'Well, it's true,' said William. 'And we don't have to go as far as that. My best friend had an accident and is in a wheelchair for the rest of her life.'

Anna's face softened. 'OK. You're right, of course. But I've had this problem for ten years and you've only had it for ten minutes. You can't imagine what it's like.'

'I mean, tomorrow all this will be yesterday's news.'

'You don't understand, do you?' She looked at him. 'They keep these photos. Every time someone writes about me, these photos will be in the papers. Newspapers last forever. I'll be *sorry* about this forever.'

The colour left William's face. He realized now that this was the end.

'Right. Fine. I *won't* be sorry, if it's all right with you. I'll always be glad you came. But you're right. You should go.'

She looked at him sadly, and then the doorbell rang again. Keeping her head down, Anna ran outside. There were shouts from the crowd of reporters and photographers. And then she was gone.

William turned to Spike. 'Was it you?' he asked.

'Well,' Spike said slowly, 'it's possible that I told one or two people in the pub.'

William sighed. 'Right.'

Chapter 9 New Hope

Summer ended and autumn leaves began to fall. William continued with his life, but he couldn't escape a feeling of emptiness. Every day was the same. He lived through that winter in a dream. Nothing seemed important. And then it was spring.

'We've got something for you,' said Honey, coming into the bookshop. Spike stood behind her in the doorway. 'You'll love me for the rest of your life.'

'What is it?' asked William, interested.

'The phone number of Anna Scott's office in London, and the one in New York. You can ring her! You think about her all the time. Now you can ring her.'

William knew Honey was trying to help. He tried to look pleased. 'Well, thank you. That's great.'

'It *is* great,' she said, smiling. 'See you tonight.'

Honey and Spike left. William looked at the piece of paper in his hand for a minute. Then, with a sigh, he threw it away.

That evening, the friends met again at Tony's restaurant. Tony's dream was at an end; his restaurant was closing.

Bella spoke for them all. 'Exactly a year ago, this man here started the finest restaurant in London.' The friends all laughed and shouted. 'But – sadly – no one ever came to eat here.'

'Just a very small problem,' said Tony, smiling.

Bella continued. 'And so, from next week, we have to find somewhere new to eat. It's a sad time.' Tony smiled again, but the smile couldn't hide his unhappiness. 'But I just want to say one more thing. Tony, don't think there's something wrong with *you*. We can't always understand the reasons why things happen. Some things succeed and others fail. Nobody knows why. Some of us get lucky, and some of us . . .'

' . . . lose our jobs,' Bernie finished.

'No!' said Bella, in surprise.

'Yes, it's true,' Bernie replied with a sigh. 'They're changing everything, and there's no place for me. Well, you know I was no good . . .'

'So we go down together!' said Tony, lifting his glass to Bernie. 'To Bernie, the worst stockbroker in the world!'

They all laughed and drank.

'I've got something to say, too,' said Honey, standing up. 'Er . . . I've decided to get married!' They all looked surprised. 'I've found myself a nice, strange-looking man. I know he'll make me happy for the rest of my life.'

'Wait a minute,' said William. 'I'm your brother and I don't know anything about this.'

'Is it someone we know?' asked Max.

Bernie looked hopeful.

'Yes. I'll tell you when the time is right,' she replied. She sat down again and the conversation turned to other subjects.

While the others were talking, Honey whispered softly to Spike, 'Er, Spike . . . It's you.'

'Me?' He looked surprised.

'Yes. What do you think?'

'Well . . . yes, great!' He smiled.

'Are there any other important things that anyone wants to say?' Max asked.

'Yes,' William said seriously. 'I want to say that I'm sorry. I'm really sorry for the way I've been for the last six months. I have, as you know, been a little unhappy.'

'A *little* unhappy? There are dead people that are more fun to be with,' laughed Max.

'But I want to make it clear that I have turned a corner. From today, I have decided to be happy!'

'So, all that business with the American is in the past now?' Max asked.

'I believe it is.' William smiled.

'You don't think about her all the time?'

'No, I don't think I do.'

'So you're not interested that she's back in London? Or that she's filming every day in Hampstead?' Max showed him a newspaper with a picture of Anna on the front page.

William sighed. 'Oh, no!'

'So you are a *little* interested, then?' said Max.

◆

The following day, William was in Hampstead. He found the place where they were filming.

'Can I help you?' asked a guard.

'Er . . . I'm looking for Anna Scott.'

'Does she know you're coming?'

'Er . . . no. No, she doesn't.'

'I'm afraid I can't let you in.'

'Oh, right. I mean, she's a friend. But . . . you . . .'

' . . . can't let you in,' repeated the guard, turning away.

Behind the guard, William saw Anna walking across the grass. She looked beautiful in a long dress and with her hair piled on top of her head. There were people all around her, ready to help her.

Suddenly, Anna looked up and saw William. Her face showed

surprise. William smiled nervously. And then she walked towards him, followed by the crowd of people.

'This is very... er...' she started, hesitantly.

'I only found out you were here yesterday.'

'I wanted to ring, but I didn't think you...' Anna continued.

'Anna, we have to go. They're ready.' It was one of the film people.

'Listen, William. It's not going well – and it's our last day.'

'Yes. Right. You're clearly very busy.'

'But wait. There are... things to say.'

'OK,' William said.

'You could drink tea. There's lots of tea.' She smiled at him, as she was taken away.

'Come and watch,' a woman said to him. 'Do you like Henry James?'

'This is a Henry James film?' he asked, remembering his conversation with Anna a year earlier.

The woman left William with Harry, a sound man.

'You can listen if you like,' Harry said, pointing to some headphones.

William put them on. Then he sat in a chair to watch the action.

Anna and another actor were making conversation, waiting for the filming. William could hear everything through the headphones.

'So I ask you when you're going to tell everyone. And you say...?' Anna said to the other actor.

' "Tomorrow will be soon enough." '

'And then I...'

'Who was that man you were talking to just now?' the other man asked.

'Oh – no one. A man from the past. I don't know what he's doing here. It's difficult.'

William's heart stopped. What *was* he doing there? He took off the headphones and gave them back to the sound man.

'Thank you, Harry.'

'Any time,' Harry smiled.

William walked away. ✓

Chapter 10 Just a Girl and a Boy

'What's happening?' Spike asked.

'I'm throwing out some old videos,' William replied. Some of them were, of course, Anna's films.

'You can't do that! These are great films. You mustn't do it! I won't let you!'

'Right. Let's talk about the money for your room . . .'

'Ah . . . right . . . I'll help you. You're right. We don't need all of them!'

The next day, at work, William was at his desk when Martin called to him.

'Excuse me, William, there's a package,' Martin said.

'Well? You work here, don't you?' he replied.

'But it's not for the shop. It's for you.'

'OK,' William sighed, getting up from his desk. 'But tell me . . . What exactly do I pay you for?'

William walked towards the front of the shop and stopped suddenly. There, in front of him, was Anna. She was dressed very simply, but was as beautiful as always.

'Hi!' she smiled.

'Hello.'

'You left . . .'

'Yes, I'm sorry. I had to leave. I was in the way.'

'Well . . . how have you been?' she asked.

'Fine,' he said. 'Everything is exactly as it was before. When they change the law, Spike and I will marry immediately. Very different from your film star life.'

'Oh, no. All that means nothing. I had no idea how meaningless it all was. But I know now.' She looked nervous. 'Yesterday was the last day of filming. I'm leaving soon and I wanted you to have this.' She pointed to a large, flat package covered in brown paper.

'Oh. Thank you. Shall I . . . ?'

'No. Don't open it now.'

'OK. Well, thank you. I don't know what it's for. But thank you.'

'I had it in my flat in New York. And I just thought . . . But I didn't know how to call you . . .' she began hesitantly. 'I was so rude to you last time. So it was in the hotel. But then – you came. So I thought . . . I thought . . .'

'What did you think?' he asked softly.

The shop door opened and Mr Smith walked in.

William looked up. 'Don't even think about it. Go away immediately!'

'Right. Sorry,' Mr Smith said in surprise, closing the door behind him.

William turned back to Anna. 'You were saying?'

'I have to go away tomorrow. And I wanted to ask you . . . Do you think I could see you a little . . . or a lot, maybe? Can you ever . . . like me again?'

William was surprised at her words. He didn't know how to reply. 'But yesterday, the other actor asked you about me. "A man from the past," you said. I heard it all through the headphones.'

'But I never tell other actors about my love life!'

Martin was back. 'Excuse me, it's your mother on the phone.'

'Tell her I'll ring later.'

'I tried that. But you said that twenty-four hours ago and she's still waiting. Her foot was purple then, and it's now turning black.'

'OK,' William sighed, walking to his desk. 'Look after Miss Scott, Martin.'

Martin smiled nervously at Anna. 'I loved you in *Ghost*. It was a wonderful film!'

'Is that right?' she said, surprised.

'Yes. What's Patrick Swayze like in real life?'

'I'm afraid I don't know him very well.'

'Oh? Wasn't he friendly when you were making the film?'

'Well . . . I'm sure he was friendly – to Demi Moore. *She* was the other star of *Ghost*.' Anna smiled.

'Oh. Right. Sorry. I've never been very clever . . .' William returned. 'Er . . . it was lovely to meet you. I love your work . . . and Demi's, of course.' And Martin left them.

'Sorry about that,' William said.

'That's OK.'

William thought very carefully and then spoke slowly and seriously. 'Anna, I'm an ordinary sort of person. I'm not often in and out of love . . .' The words were not coming easily. 'Can I just say no to your kind offer?'

Anna continued smiling, but the hurt showed in her eyes. 'Yes, that's fine. Of course . . . I . . . of course. I'll just go, then. Nice to see you.'

'Anna, the fact is . . .' He felt he must try to give words to his feelings. 'With you, I'm in real danger. My heart will never get better if it's broken again. And I know that will happen. There are too many pictures of you, everywhere, too many films. You'll continue with your life and I'll be . . . finished.'

'I see,' Anna said softly. 'That really is a real "no", isn't it?'

'I live in Notting Hill. You live in Beverly Hills. Everyone in the world knows who you are. My mother doesn't always remember my name.'

'OK. Fine. I understand.' There seemed nothing more to say. But Anna tried one last time. 'It's not real, you know . . . being famous. I'm also just a girl. Standing in front of a boy. Asking him to love her.'

William looked deeply into her eyes. Was he doing the right thing? Then she kissed him lightly.

'Bye,' she said, as she left.

♦

There were no pictures on the walls of Tony's restaurant. The kitchen equipment was gone. Chairs were piled up, waiting to go. The friends met there one last time.

'What do you think? Did I do the right thing?' William asked them.

'Of course you did,' said Honey quickly. 'I mean, she's nothing special.'

'That's right,' agreed Bella. 'And everyone knows that all actresses are crazy.'

'What do you think, Tony?' William asked.

'Never met her and never wanted to.'

'Right. Max?' William turned to his oldest friend.

'I agree with the others. And who wants to go out with someone who doesn't eat meat?'

'Great. Excellent. Thanks.' William felt happier. His decision was the right one. Then Spike arrived.

'I was called and I came. What's the problem?' he asked.

'William has just refused Anna Scott,' Honey told him.

'What? Are you crazy?' Spike shouted at William.

Bella was looking carefully at the painting next to William's chair. 'That isn't the real Chagall painting, is it?' she asked him.

'Er . . . yes. I think it is.'

Bella's eyes widened.

'And she really wanted to go out with you?' Bernie asked.

'Well . . . yes.'

'That's nice.'

'What?' asked William.

'Well, it's nice when someone wants to go out with you,' replied Bernie a little sadly.

'It was quite sweet, really,' said William, remembering. 'I mean, I know as an actress she can say lines very well. But she said – and these were her words – "I'm just a girl. Standing in front of a boy. Asking him to love her."' The room went very quiet. 'Oh, no!' William said, his head in his hands. 'I've made the wrong decision, haven't I?' He could see his friends' agreement in their eyes. 'Max, how fast is your car?'

William, Bernie, Honey and Spike jumped into Max's car.

'Where's Bella?' asked Max.

'She's not coming,' replied Honey.

'Oh yes she is. She's not missing this!' And he found Bella, picked her up and put her in the front. The wheelchair went in the back with Spike.

The London traffic was heavy, as usual, but they got to the Ritz at last. William and Bernie ran to the front desk.

'Is Miss Scott staying here?'

'No, sir. I'm afraid she isn't.' It was the man who was at the desk a year earlier.

'Or . . . er . . . Miss Flintstone?'

'No, sir. I'm afraid not.'

'Er . . . Bambi? Or . . . I don't know . . . Beavis or Butthead?'

The man at the desk shook his head. William sighed deeply. It was no good – it was too late. But as he turned away, the man spoke.

'There was a Miss Pocahontas here in room 126, but she left an hour ago. I believe she's giving a press conference at the Savoy Hotel before her flight to America.' He smiled.

William jumped up and kissed him. 'Thank you, thank you,' he shouted.

Bernie, in his excitement, kissed the man too.

Back in the car, they drove as fast as possible to the Savoy Hotel. But the traffic was moving slowly, and at one crossroads they came to a complete stop. Time passed and they all got more and more nervous.

Spike jumped out of the car. 'I'll get us through,' he shouted, shutting the door. And then he was in the middle of the road, stopping cars and buses and making a path for Max's car. 'Go, go, go!' he shouted.

'I love you,' laughed Honey out of the window, as the car shot off towards the Savoy.

'Excuse me. Where's the press conference?' William asked the man at the desk.

'Can I see your press card?'

William quickly showed him a card.

'That's a video club card, sir.'

'Yes, I write for the club's magazine.'

'I'm sorry, sir . . .'

Bella arrived at the front desk, pushed by Honey. 'He's with me,' she said.

'And you are . . . ?'

' . . . writing about the best London hotels for people in wheelchairs,' she said, smiling.

The man looked at her for a minute, and then sighed. 'It's in the Lancaster Room. I'm afraid you're very late.'

'Run,' Honey shouted to William.

The Lancaster Room was crowded with reporters and photographers. At the front sat Anna behind a long table, looking a little sad. Jeremy, from the film company, was next to her.

'Yes . . . you, Dominic,' said Jeremy, pointing to a reporter.

'How much longer are you staying in Britain, Miss Scott?'

'No time at all. I fly out tonight,' answered Anna.

'And that's why we have to stop soon,' said Jeremy. 'Any last questions?'

A number of hands went up and he pointed to one.

'You've decided not make another film for a year. Is this because there's talk about Jeff and another famous actress?'

'No,' she replied, simply.

'Do you believe the stories?'

'It's really not my business now. But I will say this. Stories about Jeff and women are usually true.' She smiled.

The next question came from a reporter standing next to William.

'Last time you were here, there were photos of you and a young Englishman. So what was that about?'

'He was just a friend. And I think we're still friends,' she said slowly.

William's heart was jumping. Could he speak? Could he say what he wanted to say? And then his hand was up and Jeremy was pointing at him.

'Yes. Miss Scott. Is there any chance of you and this young man being . . . more than friends?'

Anna looked up at the questioner. She saw that it was William.

'I thought so. But no, I was told not,' she said quietly.

'And if this man . . .' William started.

Jeremy spoke. 'No. It's just one question each.'

'No. Let him,' Anna said. She turned back to William. 'What were you saying?'

William continued. 'If . . . this person . . .'

'His name was Thacker,' said one of the reporters helpfully.

'Thank you,' William smiled. 'If this Mr Thacker gets down on his knees and asks you to think again . . . what then?'

Max, Bella, Bernie and Honey all waited, open-mouthed, for her answer.

'I think my answer will be . . . yes!' Her smile lit up the room.

'That's excellent news. The readers of *Horse and Hound* will be very happy.'

Anna turned to Jeremy and whispered something.

'Dominic, would you like to ask your question again?' said Jeremy, pointing to the reporter.

'Yes. Miss Scott, how long are you planning to stay in Britain?'

Anna looked at William questioningly. He returned her look, smiled and mouthed the word 'yes'.

'For a very long time,' smiled Anna.

Suddenly, the reporters realized what was happening. They crowded round William, asking him questions. Photographers took pictures. Max and Bella kissed. Bernie kissed a woman standing next to him. Everyone was smiling and laughing.

Spike arrived at last, red-faced from running. 'What happened?' he asked Honey.

She put her arms around him and held him tightly. 'It was good, Spike. It was so good.'

♦

How did it all end, this love story between the biggest film star in the world and an ordinary bookseller from Notting Hill? Well, it is too early to say. But the signs are good.

The wedding was a quiet one with family and close friends. Tony made a wonderful cake. Max danced wildly around the dance floor, looking like James Bond in his white dinner jacket. Honey's legs didn't reach the floor as she danced in Spike's arms. And Martin stood at the side, smiling nervously. Everyone had a good time.

Soon after the wedding, William went with Anna to the opening night of her Henry James film. As they stepped out of the car in front of the cinema, people screamed with excitement. Photographers pushed forward to get the best picture for the next day's newspaper. To William, all this was new and strange. But Anna held his hand tightly and guided him through the crowds.

We leave the happy lovers on a sunny day a year later, in a garden in Notting Hill. All around them are signs of life and love. Children are playing, watched by their mothers. One is holding her new baby. An older woman walks past with her husband. They are smiling and talking softly. On a simple wooden seat, William sits reading. Anna is lying next to him, looking out over the gardens. She looks calm and happy. From time to time, her hand moves slowly over the baby growing inside her.

ACTIVITIES

Chapters 1–3

Before you read

1 Read the Introduction to this book – or remember the film – and answer these questions.

- **a** What kind of story is *Notting Hill*?
- **b** What nationalities are William and Anna?
- **c** What are their jobs?

2 Anna Scott is very rich, successful and famous. What do you think her life is like? What parts of her life will she enjoy? What will she find difficult? Do you think she has a lot of friends? Why (not)?

3 Look at the titles of the chapters in this book. Do you think that Anna and William will find love together? Will they have problems? Give reasons for your answers.

4 Look at the Word List at the back of the book. Find words to complete these sentences.

- **a** He wore a .... and a pair of .... when he swam under water.
- **b** She .... at the computer .... until her eyes hurt.
- **c** Spike is William's .... and lives in his house.
- **d** Anna .... when the .... rang. She didn't want to speak to the .... again.
- **e** People were surprised when the man stepped into the street. He was wearing only his ....
- **f** She didn't want to eat in the hotel restaurant, so she called .... for food.
- **g** Spike's hair was a .... and his clothes were dirty.
- **h** 'Put your clothes on!' she said. 'You can't walk around ....!'

While you read

5 In which order do these happen? Number the sentences 1–8.

- **a** Anna kisses William. .....
- **b** Spike remembers the name 'Flintstone'. .....

c Anna buys a book in William's shop. .....
d Anna invites William to have tea with her. .....
e Anna gets orange juice on her clothes. .....
f William speaks to Anna on the phone. .....
g Anna goes to William's house. .....
h Anna leaves a message for William. .....

After you read

6 Who is speaking? What are they talking about?
  a 'Can you help me with an important decision?'
  b 'We've got a camera in this part of the shop.'
  c 'I haven't got a book down my trousers.'
  d 'Perhaps one day a famous person *will* come in.'
  e 'What are you doing?'
  f 'Have you got any books by Dickens?'
  g 'No clean clothes.'
  h 'I'm a friend of Anna Scott's.'
  i 'We have nobody here of that name.'
  j 'Yes, but I'm a little busy today.'

7 Discuss these questions with another student.
  a Is William married or single? Why is his business not successful? Is he kind to other people? Would you like to meet him?
  b What does Spike look like? Why is he at William's house? What kind of person is he?
  c Why does Anna use a different name at the hotel? What name does she use? Do you think her life is hard? Why (not)?

Chapters 4–6

Before you read

8 Discuss these questions.
  a What kind of hotel is the Ritz, do you think? Will it be big or small, expensive or cheap? What will Anna's rooms be like?
  b What do you think will happen when William meets Anna at the Ritz?

9 What do you know about these people?
  a Martin   b Mr Smith

While you read

10 Are these sentences true (T) or false (F)?

a William is a reporter for *Horse and Hound* magazine. .....

b William's friends are surprised when he brings Anna to Honey's party. .....

c Honey is William's older sister. .....

d Bernie is very successful in his job. .....

e Bella can't walk because of an accident. .....

f Bella and Max have a child. .....

g After the meal, Anna and William go to a garden. .....

h The men in the Japanese restaurant say unkind things about Anna. .....

i William doesn't know that Anna has a boyfriend. .....

j William says he is happy to clear away Jeff's plates. .....

After you read

11 Answer these questions.

a Why does William tell Karen that he works for a magazine?

b Why are the other actors not very pleased with William's questions?

c Why does Honey want Anna to marry William?

d Why has Bernie had a bad day at work?

e Why do the friends scream after William and Anna leave?

f Who does Jeff think that William is?

g How does William feel when he leaves the Ritz for the second time?

12 Describe the good and bad parts of these people's lives. Who has the most problems? Who would *you* give the last piece of cake to?

a Bernie **b** William **c** Bella **d** Anna

13 Work in pairs. Have this conversation.

Student A: You are William. It is the day after you met Anna's boyfriend. Explain to Max what happened.

Student B: You are Max. Listen to William and ask him questions.

Chapters 7–8

Before you read

14 What do you think of when you think about these people? Write one or two words for each person. Then compare your answers with another student's. Are they the same?

a Spike **c** Bella **e** Bernie
b Max **d** Honey **f** Jeff

15 Discuss these questions. What do you think?

a Will William try to see Anna again? Why (not)?
b Max decides to introduce William to some young women. Is this a good idea? Why (not)?
c Anna is back in the United States. Do you think she is happy? Why (not)?

While you read

16 Choose the right ending for each sentence.

a Tessa	gets a surprise in the bathroom.
b Keziah	was William's girlfriend, years ago.
c Bella	thinks Spike spoke to the newspapers.
d Anna	only eats 'dead' fruit.
e The newspapers	has opened his first restaurant.
f Spike	fill the street outside William's house.
g Anna	wants to get away from the reporters.
h Tony	enjoys getting drunk.
i The reporters	are full of pictures of Anna.

After you read

17 Complete these sentences.

a William doesn't read *Hello!* magazine, so he …
b In Notting Hill there are a lot of street names with 'Kensington' in them, so Tessa …
c William has always been unlucky in love, so he ...
d There are crowds of reporters around her hotel, so Anna ...

e Anna is going to start work on a new film, so William ...

f Reporters and photographers arrive at William's house, so Anna ...

g William tells Spike not to go outside the house, so Spike ...

h Spike met some friends in the pub, so he ...

18 Work in pairs. Have these conversations.

a *Student A*: You are Spike. You are in the pub with a friend. Tell him about Anna Scott and your visit to the bathroom.

Student B: You are Spike's friend. At first, you don't believe his story. When you do, ask for more information.

b *Student A*: You are Spike's friend. Phone a reporter, and try to sell information about Anna Scott.

Student B: You are a reporter. Ask a lot of questions – and try not to agree to a large payment.

Chapters 9–10

Before you read

19 What do you think? In the next two chapters, who:

a closes his business?

Bernie	Tony	William	Max

b decides to get married?

Honey	Bernie	Jeff	Tony

c finds Anna making a film?

Honey	William	Spike	Max

d sends William an expensive gift?

Tessa	Keziah	Bella	Anna

e refuses to see Anna again?

Honey	Max	William	Jeff

20 Do you think William and Anna will be together at the end of this story? Why (not)? What will happen? Discuss your ideas with another student.

While you read

21 Circle the best words to complete these sentences.

a William feels *empty / happy* without Anna.

b William *phones / doesn't phone* Anna's office.

c Bernie has *left / lost* his job.

d Spike *knew / didn't know* that Honey loved him.

e Max shows William a picture of Anna in *Los Angeles / London.*

f William and Anna are both *angry / nervous* when they meet in Hampstead.

g William *enjoys / doesn't enjoy* the conversation that he hears through the headphones.

h Anna gives William a *painting / book*.

i At the meeting in the bookshop, William decides that he *wants / doesn't want* to be with Anna.

j By the end of their meeting at Tony's, William's friends decide that Anna *loves / doesn't love* him.

k At the press conference, Anna *agrees / doesn't agree* to stay in London.

After you read

22 Who is the speaker talking about?

a 'the worst stockbroker in the world.'

b 'a nice, strange-looking man.'

c 'There are dead people that are more fun to be with.'

d 'You don't think about her all the time?'

e 'Oh – no one. A man from the past.'

f 'Her foot was purple then, and it's now turning black.'

g 'Wasn't he friendly when you were making the film?'

h '*She* was the other star of *Ghost*.'

i 'She's nothing special.'

j 'She's not missing this!'

23 What do you remember? Why are these things important in the story?

a a blue front door

b a glass of orange juice

c Flintstone

d *Horse and Hound*

e $15,000,000

f a wooden garden seat

g a Chagall painting

h Henry James's *The Wings of the Dove*

24 Discuss these questions.

a Do you think that William and Anna's marriage will be successful?

b What do you think they each want from the marriage?

c What difficulties will there be for each of them?

25 Work with another student. Decide what happens to these people after the end of the story.

a Spike and Honey

b Bernie

c Max and Bella

d Tony

Writing

26 You are one of the reporters outside William's house when he comes out in his underpants. Write a report for the next day's newspaper.

27 Imagine that you are William, before the end of the story. You love Anna but you don't want to see her again. Write a letter to her and explain your reasons.

28 You are a magazine reporter and you are going to the press conference at the Savoy Hotel. Write a list of questions for Anna about Jeff; her films; the young English man; her feelings about the press.

29 Why does William love Anna? What does Anna love about William? Explain why they married.

30 Imagine that you are Anna. You are telling a friend what you love about William. Write down what you will say.

31 The wedding between William and Anna is the most exciting one this year. You have been asked to write about it for a national newspaper. Describe the wedding and the party. Write about as many of the guests as you can.

32 Describe the place Notting Hill for a report in a travel magazine. Tell visitors what they will see there. Why will they like it? Use the Internet or travel books and find out about other exciting places in London, near Notting Hill, for visitors.

33 You are Honey. It is twelve months after the end of the story. Bernie is now living in the United States. Write a letter to him. Tell him what has happened to you and Spike, William and Anna, and your other friends.

34 Look at the last part of Chapter 10. Think about a different – less happy – ending to the story. Make notes, and then write another ending to the chapter.

35 Write about three of the people in this book. Describe:

a what you like (or dislike) about them.

b why they are important to the story.

Answers for the Activities in this book are available from the Pearson English Readers website. A free Activity Worksheet is also available from the website. Activity worksheets are part of the Pearson English Readers Teacher Support Programme, which also includes Progress tests and Graded Reader Guidelines. For more information, please visit: www.pearsonenglishreaders.com